This Thing Has a Name

By

Amanda Bacon-Davis

Illustrated by

Jinjer Markley

© 2022

To My Ella Rain

You are my greatest gift and my greatest teacher.
It's an honor to be your mommy.
I love watching your magic
grow bigger and stronger every day.
Thank you for showing the world…
what it looks like to be brave.

Feelings, oh feelings,
I have them all day
Sometimes they change
And sometimes they stay

I can feel brave
Fearless and bold
Just like a star
Trying new things, even doing some old

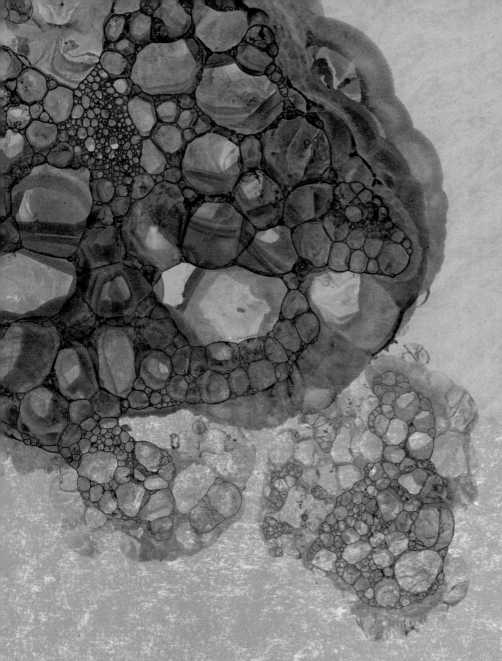

But then there are times
I don't feel like a star
Life can get messy
Even scary or bizarre

That feeling I get
When I don't feel at all
I go numb, feel dumb
I've hit a big wall

My tummy might ache
My eyes might go fuzzy
My body won't move
Until somebody loves me

But the people who love me
They wrap me up tight
To calm these big feelings
And hold me just right

My mind goes in circles
Nighttime's the worst!
Thoughts are so scattered
My brain might just burst!

The people who love me
They do understand
They tell me I'm normal
while holding my hand

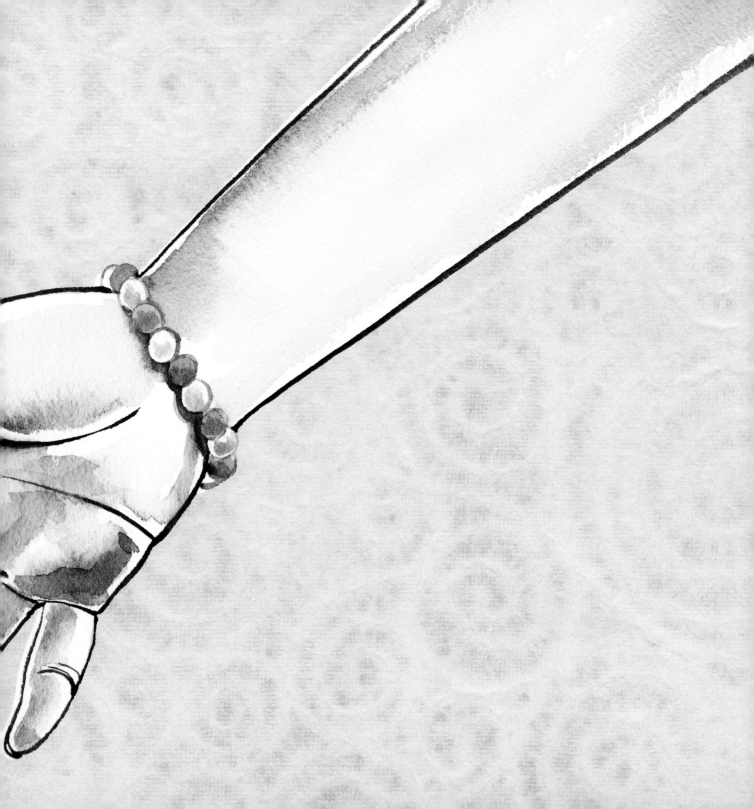

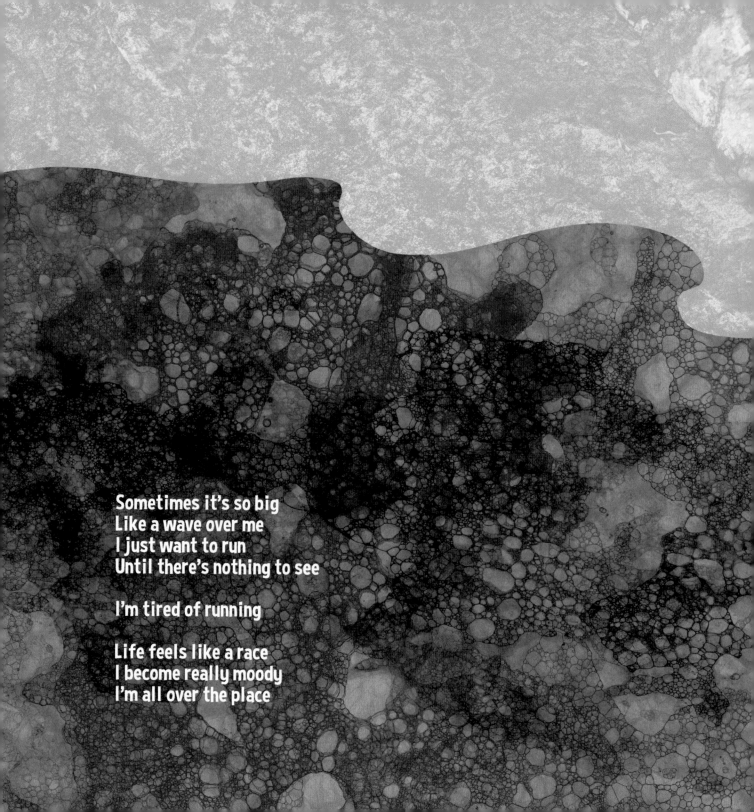

Sometimes it's so big
Like a wave over me
I just want to run
Until there's nothing to see

I'm tired of running

Life feels like a race
I become really moody
I'm all over the place

But the people who love me
They tell me it's true
No matter how I'm feeling

They say, "we love you"

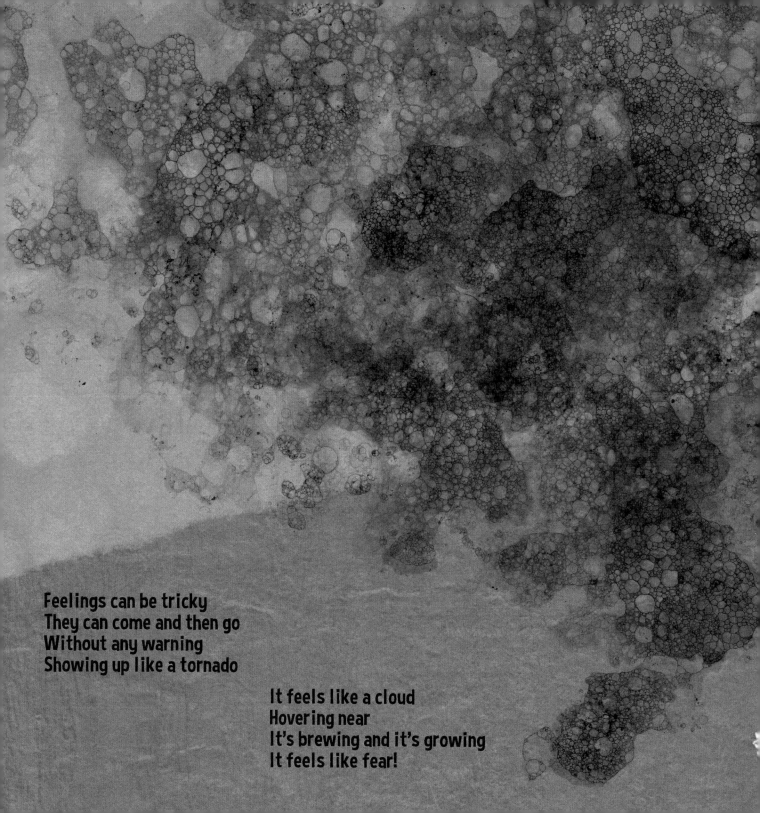

Feelings can be tricky
They can come and then go
Without any warning
Showing up like a tornado

It feels like a cloud
Hovering near
It's brewing and it's growing
It feels like fear!

I think I'll escape...
I'll get on a train

To run far away

Away from this pain

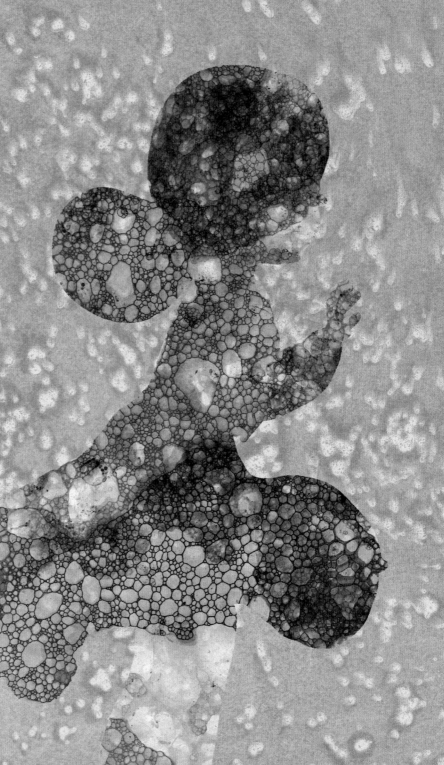

This fear that comes
In all shapes and all sizes
Brings with it more feelings
and unwanted surprises

It can trick my mind
Popping up uninvited
Until I'm too tired
To fight it and fight it

These things that I am feeling
I can't quite explain
But I just learned that this thing,

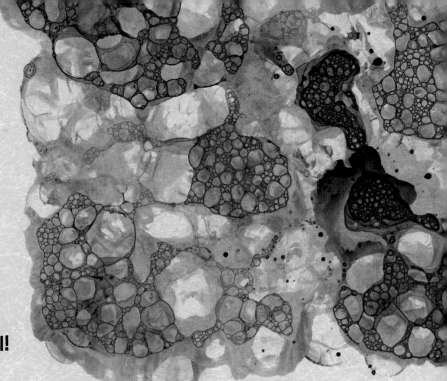

The people who love me
They say that it's real
It's called anxiety
And I can learn how to heal!

Anxiety means there's a boo-boo inside
It's not something we see
But we know that it's there...
The important thing is,

I feel safe and can share

One thing I know
And I'm just learning how
Is I have so many tools
To handle this now

There are so many ways
I can help myself heal

I can count to ten,

practice my breathing

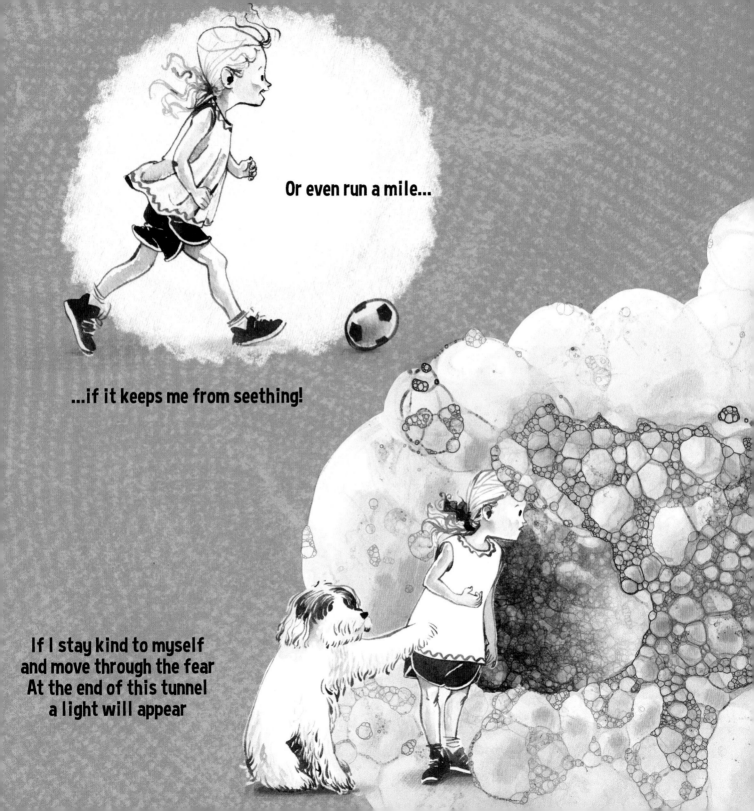

Or even run a mile...

...if it keeps me from seething!

If I stay kind to myself
and move through the fear
At the end of this tunnel
a light will appear

Sometimes it comes fast
and sometimes it's slow
But a little self-compassion
Makes me stronger, I know

The only way out
Is to go all the way in
I must feel all these feelings
to let the healing begin

The people that love me know when
I'm not feeling myself
I'm still me inside,
and that's all that counts

So, I won't run away
I won't jump on a train
I'll do something I love
Like dance in the rain!!

The people that love me
say I'm full of AMAZE.
Because I'm working on healing...
New trails I must blaze!

They say I am brave and
Full of strong courage
To have all of these feelings
And not get discouraged

The people who love me
Only ask me one thing
Keep working on me and
My special healing

And to please just remember
Because it will always be true
That no matter what...
They'll always say, "We love you"

Different Ways I Can Help Heal Myself

Please remember the most important thing is to be kind to yourself and know that the people around you want to help. Also, what works for you, might not work for someone else - because we are all different.

Some ways that work for our family:

* Practice counting slowly to 10, and then slowly backwards again. Focusing only on the numbers, and the speed at which you are counting, to let your thoughts drift away.

* Stand like Superman or Superwoman for 3 minutes! Have your Loved One set a timer. Stand with your legs shoulder width apart, with your hands on your hips, your back and head nice and tall, look from side to side, while keeping your head high and smiling (even if you don't feel like it…it can help).

* Drink freezing cold water. Brrrrr…be careful not to drink too slow, but don't drink it too fast (we don't want you to get a brain freeze!). Drinking cold water can help calm our insides.

* Move your body. Running really fast, somewhere safe like your backyard to get energy out can help. Sometimes yelling while running can help too. Just make sure you let your Loved One know what you need to do, so they can make sure you stay safe.

* Come up with some positive affirmations. Affirmations are positive statements you can say about yourself. You can do this alone, standing in front of a mirror, looking at yourself (in the eyes), and saying them out loud. You can also do this with your Loved One, looking at them, or having them hold you. Here are some example affirmations:

I am loved
I am safe
I am healthy
I am strong
I am brave
I can do anything I set my mind to
I am proud of myself

Find more affirmations at **thisthinghasaname.com**

◆   Journal your feelings – you can write or draw them. Be as specific as you can with the time of day and what you were doing when these feelings popped up. This can help you learn what might be bringing these feelings up, but it's also a helpful way to quietly get your feelings out.

◆   Ask for help. Your Loved One's want to make your inside boo-boo better. Maybe all you need is to be held tight for a little while and told everything is going to be okay (because it is, even if in the moment it doesn't feel that way). We call that "loving time" at our house. Snuggle up with your Loved One and relax.

◆   Find something that will make you giggle and feel silly. Laughing makes our brains feel better.

◆   Dance! With music, without music. Alone, or with a Loved One. Move your body, be silly and have fun, even if you have to push yourself a little to get going. (Hint: If you are watching TV, get up and dance at the TV commercials to the music that is playing!)

◆   Take a Loved One with you and visit some nature. It can be the woods, the beach, a lake, anywhere peaceful that changes your everyday scenery.

◆   Make sure you are talking with someone who you feel safe with, it could be a parent, aunt or uncle, a friend, a teacher, or a therapist. The important thing is you feel safe to share, which means you will not be judged or get in any trouble for whatever feelings you are having.

◆   Listen to mindful mediation by visiting **thisthinghasaname.com** for links just for you!

For more ways you can help heal yourself and links to other resources please visit: **thisthing-hasaname.com**.

BONUS! If you have ideas of what works for you that are missing from this list, we'd love to hear them! Please have your Loved One share it with us by emailing **info@thisthinghasaname.com**, so we can keep helping other people, just like you! Remember...You are not alone, and you are perfectly perfect with any feelings you may have.

To The People Who Love

Full disclosure…I am not a doctor, I am not a therapist, I am in no way a medical professional. I am a mother and a human, who has held my own battles of anxiety and depression, while holding the battle for others, most importantly, my daughter.

For many years, I thought outside of my family, I was alone in dealing with this monster that would come and attack my daughter at any given moment. At the exact time I wrote this book, I quickly learned I was far from alone, and that feeling was like being wrapped in a warm blanket.

There's an entire community of us out there, loving children with anxiety. Many of us are silently suffering, for any number of reasons – not wanting our child to be the 'weird' kid at school, or wanting to admit this is our reality, or not knowing that what we are witnessing…is even anxiety, or maybe - we are just too tired to share it. This is real and this is hard, but you are not alone. In fact, you are a hero.

As a community, we need to normalize these feelings for our children, big and small, and help them learn to manage and cope in healthy ways with their feelings. This is not easy in the world we live in today, as there seems to be a reason to be anxious hiding around every corner.

It truly does take a village, so I encourage you to create one in any way you can. That could mean your family, your school system, or your friends. We are starting an online community at **thisthinghasaname.com** for you to come and share your story, your hurt and your triumphs, or to just read what other people have to say, and know you are not alone.

Every child, little or big, will experience anxiety in their life. For some it will be fleeting, for others it will be an everyday battle. Our job must be to normalize these feelings. To let children know their feelings are valid and help them learn positive coping tools that work for them. Tools they can eventually use on their own, while loving them when they feel the most unlovable.

My family's story is the same as your family's, and yet completely different. You can read about my family's story at **thisthinghasaname.com.**

Thank you for taking the time to read this book with your little one. I hope it helps bring calm and peace, in knowing that this thing…this thing has a name – ***and this thing can be tamed.***

All my love and support,

Amanda

About the Author:

Amanda Bacon-Davis is a successful businesswoman, entrepreneur, and a proud advocate for supporting the mental health community.
She has a beautiful daughter, Ella Rain, two amazing bonus kids (who are actually wonderful adults), and the most loving husband in the world.
Amanda and her family live on the Seacoast of New Hampshire with their two dogs, Dog-Dog (featured in the book) and Halo. When she is not writing, Amanda's favorite thing to do is belly-laugh with her family.

Made in the USA
Coppell, TX
10 June 2023

17911388R00024